10 MINUTE MOMENTS

THE

BASICS

EXPLORING THE BOOK OF JOHN
10 MINUTES AT A TIME

JOSHUA
GRIFFIN

simply for students

YouthMinistry.com/TOGETHER

10 Minute Moments: The Basics
Exploring the Book of John 10 Minutes at a Time

© 2013 Joshua Griffin

group.com
simplyyouthministry.com

Credits
Author: Joshua Griffin
Executive Developer: Nadim Najm
Chief Creative Officer: Joani Schultz
Editor: Rob Cunningham
Cover Art and Production: Riley Hall

Unless otherwise noted, all Scripture quotations are taken from the *Holy Bible*, New Living Translation, copyright © 1996, 2004, 2007 by Tyndale House Foundation. Used by permission of Tyndale House Publishers, Inc., Carol Stream, Illinois 60188. All rights reserved.

ISBN 978-1-4707-0101-7

10 9 8 7 6 5 4 3 2 1   20 19 18 17 16 15 14 13

Printed in the United States of America.

CONTENTS

I'm excited to journey with you for the next 30 days!

As we read God's Word together, I challenge you to apply it to your life and journal some of your thoughts along the way. Just 10 minutes will change each day—and a whole bunch of those days strung together will change your life forever.

I'm most excited about this resource because I think it will help you grow significantly in understanding some of the basics of our faith. No matter where you are in your spiritual journey, there are some great truths that we can apply to our lives. Here's what will happen as we study the book of John together:

If you're a new Christ-follower... you'll be introduced to who God is, what God has done, and how God's Spirit enables you to live a new life in him. You'll walk away with a fresh understanding about God from one of the clearest and most-read books of the Bible.

If you're looking for a refresher on the basics... this will help you if you've been away from church for a while or aren't a "church kid." This study will be a perfect way for you to get a renewed perspective on the fundamental beliefs and teachings of Jesus.

If you're a sold-out follower of Jesus... some of these passages will no doubt be familiar to you, but I hope to challenge you into a deeper understanding of all God has done for us and push you to be even more of a dedicated disciple.

Blessings as you study God's Word!

Joshua Griffin

DAY 1

A LIGHT IN THE DARKNESS

When I was younger, my family toured one of the largest caves in the United States. About halfway through the cave, the tour guide told us to stop and proceeded to turn off all of the lights. It was pitch black—so dark you literally couldn't see your hand in front of your face. I know this because I tried!

After a few moments, the tour guide shone a small flashlight and pierced the darkness, much to the relief of our group. I can only imagine what it would have been like to try to complete our tour without the light. Even that small little flashlight made a world of difference!

2 MINUTES

Scripture to read: John 1:1-5

In the beginning the Word already existed.
  The Word was with God,
  and the Word was God.
He existed in the beginning with God.
God created everything through him,
  and nothing was created except through him.
The Word gave life to everything that was created,
  and his life brought light to everyone.
The light shines in the darkness,
  and the darkness can never extinguish it.

Questions to think about

- This passage says that God never had a beginning—that God always was. Do you have confidence in knowing that God has a great plan for your life? Why or why not?

- Has there ever been a time when you experienced complete darkness? How did it make you feel?

- Is there some area in your life that you are resisting in giving over to the Lord? Are you struggling with trusting the Lord completely?

How difficult would it be to navigate a world without light? The light of Jesus Christ will never go out because it lives inside of us. As followers of Jesus, once we accept him as our Savior, we have a light that can never be distinguished. Shine bright this week to your friends!

Hanging out with God

Go into the darkest place in your house and experience darkness for a few moments. Then open the door and be thankful for the light! Celebrate that God's light has pierced the darkness, and commit to shine the light of Jesus to others today.

YOUR TURN

This space is here for you to jot down some thoughts, write out a prayer, draw a picture, or do whatever you want to help you remember your 10-minute moment:

DAY 2

PICTURE THIS

I had the privilege of seeing one of the most famous paintings in the world in person: the Mona Lisa. It was incredible to see such a monumental work of art. But if I'm being completely honest, I don't think I appreciated it as much as I was supposed to. To me, it looked like an average painting of a woman who wasn't very happy in the first place! Obviously, I failed to understand (and still do) the significance of the apparently groundbreaking piece of art by Leonardo da Vinci.

God has given us a beautiful piece of art called baptism, and it is important to understand its significance. This is a symbol of Jesus' death, burial, and resurrection! Baptism is a step of obedience and shows the world that you are a follower of Jesus.

2 MINUTES

Scripture to read: John 1:29-34

The next day John saw Jesus coming toward him and said, "Look! The Lamb of God who takes away the sin of the world! He is the one I was talking about when I said, 'A man is coming after me who is far greater than I am, for he existed long before me.' I did not recognize him as the Messiah, but I have been baptizing with water so that he might be revealed to Israel."

Then John testified, "I saw the Holy Spirit descending like a dove from heaven and resting upon him. I didn't know he was the one, but when God sent me to baptize with water, he told me, 'The one on whom you see the Spirit descend and rest is the one who will baptize with the Holy Spirit.' I saw this happen to Jesus, so I testify that he is the Chosen One of God."

Questions to think about

- Have you ever been baptized? Why or why not?

- If you are a follower of Jesus, God's Spirit lives inside of you. How have you lived that like (or failed to live like that) so far this week?

- In other parts of the Bible, we are called God's masterpiece. How does this make you feel about the way you view yourself?

Hanging out with God

Spend some time walking around the room you are in and looking at any artwork on the walls. (If the room doesn't have any artwork on the walls, find a room that does.) Why were those pieces chosen? Is there significance in those pictures, photographs, or paintings?

The Bible says that Jesus takes our sins away and that we are washed clean by Christ. Baptism is the symbol of an incredible moment where we go from a fallen and broken life, to a new life in him. It doesn't mean that we suddenly become perfect or that things are going to be easy! The best part about baptism is that when we choose Jesus, God gives us his Spirit to live inside of us and guide us through our lives.

Spend a little bit of time reflecting on this awesome gift of salvation. Celebrate the time in your life when you were baptized—or ask your parents or leader about a time when you, too, can be baptized!

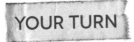

This space is here for you to jot down some thoughts, write out a prayer, draw a picture, or do whatever you want to help you remember your 10-minute moment:

DAY 3

MIRACLE MAN

The Bible records all sorts of miracles that Jesus did during his earthly ministry. He healed the blind, fed thousands of people with a single lunch, told people to stand when their legs were lame, and healed incurable diseases, such as leprosy. Needless to say, Jesus performed some pretty incredible miracles. This story is about his very first one!

2 MINUTES

Scripture to read: John 2:6-11

Standing nearby were six stone water jars, used for Jewish ceremonial washing. Each could hold twenty to thirty gallons. Jesus told the servants, "Fill the jars with water." When the jars had been filled, he said, "Now dip some out, and take it to the master of ceremonies." So the servants followed his instructions.

When the master of ceremonies tasted the water that was now wine, not knowing where it had come from (though, of course, the servants knew), he called the bridegroom over. "A host always serves the best wine first," he said. "Then, when everyone has had a lot to drink, he brings out the less expensive wine. But you have kept the best until now!"

This miraculous sign at Cana in Galilee was the first time Jesus revealed his glory. And his disciples believed in him.

5 MINUTES

Questions to think about

- Why do you think Jesus performed this miracle or any other miracle?

- Do you ever have doubts in your faith? Can you imagine what the disciples must have felt when they saw Jesus performing miracles like this one?

- What kind of miracle do you need from Jesus in your life?

3 MINUTES

Hanging out with God

Obedience is key to your walk with Christ. You need to trust what he says, even when it doesn't make sense. Ask anyone who has followed Jesus for any amount of time: God doesn't always make sense. But you can trust him! God has an eternal scope that is far beyond yours, an understanding of his will and plan that we can't fathom. Take the few remaining moments today and talk to God about trusting him with a few areas where you're having trouble understanding what he is up to right now.

YOUR TURN

This space is here for you to jot down some thoughts, write out a prayer, draw a picture, or do whatever you want to help you remember your 10-minute moment:

DAY 4

RISE UP

I remember having lots of different animals in my family growing up: our dog Peeve, the guinea pig Alfonzo…my little sister Lyssa. Seriously though, my favorite pet we ever had was our goldfish. I won him at a church carnival, and he only lived for about two hours. I never even had a chance to give him a name! I'm not going to lie to you: This was pretty tough for me as a little kid.

Death is a reality in life. It has happened or will happen to everyone. There is good news for us, though! The Bible tells us that the power of God in Jesus conquered death! Jesus even came back to life to show us that death has been defeated through him!

2 MINUTES

Scripture to read: John 2:18-22

But the Jewish leaders demanded, "What are you doing? If God gave you authority to do this, show us a miraculous sign to prove it." "All right," Jesus replied. "Destroy this temple, and in three days I will raise it up."

"What!" they exclaimed. "It has taken forty-six years to build this Temple, and you can rebuild it in three days?" But when Jesus said "this temple," he meant his own body. After he was raised from the dead, his disciples remembered he had said this, and they believed both the Scriptures and what Jesus had said.

Questions to think about

- What do you think it must have been like for the disciples to see Jesus again after he had died?

- Are there areas in your life where you feel like you are still dead? Do you feel that God needs to give you new life?

- What do your friends see when they look at your life?

Jesus came back to life from the dead. This in and of itself is a beautiful picture of our new life in him. We were dead in our sins and brought back to live a new life. Live like it today!

Hanging out with God

The Bible says that the same power that raised Christ from the dead lives in you. (See Romans 8:11 if you don't believe me!) Today you have a chance to show the world that Jesus is alive by living a life of faith. Every moment of your life is an opportunity for others to see that Jesus is still alive. Jesus lived, died, came back to life, and went to heaven nearly 2,000 years ago—but lives inside of you if you are a Christ-follower and can be seen by others right now. I wonder what your friends at school will see in you today?

YOUR TURN

This space is here for you to jot down some thoughts, write out a prayer, draw a picture, or do whatever you want to help you remember your 10-minute moment:

DAY 5

BORN THIS WAY

I was there for the birth of all four of my children. These were absolutely astonishing moments that were incredibly beautiful and totally disturbing, simultaneously. And being the guy, I think I had the easy part! But something wonderful happened: New life entered the world.

I was so proud of my sons. I was overflowing with love for my daughter. I can't believe how my heart expanded with love for each one of them in the instant that they were born. I know that God feels the same about you!

2 MINUTES

Scripture to read: John 3:1-7

There was a man named Nicodemus, a Jewish religious leader who was a Pharisee. After dark one evening, he came to speak with Jesus. "Rabbi," he said, "we all know that God has sent you to teach us. Your miraculous signs are evidence that God is with you."

Jesus replied, "I tell you the truth, unless you are born again, you cannot see the Kingdom of God."

"What do you mean?" exclaimed Nicodemus. "How can an old man go back into his mother's womb and be born again?"

Jesus replied, "I assure you, no one can enter the Kingdom of God without being born of water and the Spirit. Humans can reproduce only human life, but the Holy Spirit gives birth to spiritual life. So don't be surprised when I say, 'You must be born again.'"

Questions to think about

- How much strength do you think it took for Nicodemus to come to Jesus and ask these questions?

- Have you been "born again," as Jesus described in this passage? Have you trusted Christ as your Savior? Do you have a new spiritual life in him?

- Can anyone have eternal life without being "born again"? Why or why not?

Hanging out with God

Ask your parents what it was like when you were born, or try to remember them telling you that story. Your birthday is usually a big deal with cake and presents. How much greater is your spiritual birthday when you were "born again" through Jesus Christ? The best present you could ever receive is the new and eternal life that is freely given when you choose to follow Jesus.

Reflect today on the love of a father in the delivery room when his child is born. Imagine how much God loves you as his son or daughter, too!

This space is here for you to jot down some thoughts, write out a prayer, draw a picture, or do whatever you want to help you remember your 10-minute moment:

DAY 6

THE MOST FAMOUS VERSE IN THE WORLD

It is the most famous verse in the Bible. It is the most memorized verse in the Bible and has been memorized by millions. It is held up in the end zone of every NFL football game that has ever been played. It was written on the eye black of Tim Tebow.

It is John 3:16.

2 MINUTES

Scripture to read: John 3:16-21

"For God loved the world so much that he gave his one and only Son, so that everyone who believes in him will not perish but have eternal life. God sent his Son into the world not to judge the world, but to save the world through him.

"There is no judgment against anyone who believes in him. But anyone who does not believe in him has already been judged for not believing in God's one and only Son. And the judgment is based on this fact: God's light came into the world, but people loved the darkness more than the light, for their actions were evil. All who do evil hate the light and refuse to go near it for fear their sins will be exposed. But those who do what is right come to the light so others can see that they are doing what God wants."

5 MINUTES

Questions to think about

- Have you even felt judged by someone else? How did that make you feel?

- This passage says that anyone who believes can have eternal life. Really? Who do you think is excluded from God's love?

- These verses talk about loving darkness more than light— where is this true in your life? What are you doing about it?

Have you ever memorized John 3:16? Take some time today to reflect on this verse that may be familiar to you, and try to memorize it if it isn't!

3 MINUTES

Hanging out with God

Sometimes a familiar verse in the Bible is one we tend to move past quickly or skim over. I do this all of the time—I think, "I know that already" or "Yup, I've got that one" when in reality I might be missing something really important. Take another second today to read over today's Scripture, and look for (and maybe underline) something you may have missed!

YOUR TURN

This space is here for you to jot down some thoughts, write out a prayer, draw a picture, or do whatever you want to help you remember your 10-minute moment:

DAY 7

WORSHIP ME

Some people worship cars. Other people worship their status or piles of money. If you look around, I think it is safe to say that most people struggle with worshipping themselves!

From the beginning of time people have worshipped something—and the passage you are reading today points toward whom and how we should worship.

2 MINUTES

Scripture to read: John 4:21-26

Jesus replied, "Believe me, dear woman, the time is coming when it will no longer matter whether you worship the Father on this mountain or in Jerusalem. You Samaritans know very little about the one you worship, while we Jews know all about him, for salvation comes through the Jews. But the time is coming—indeed it's here now—when true worshipers will worship the Father in spirit and in truth. The Father is looking for those who will worship him that way. For God is Spirit, so those who worship him must worship in spirit and in truth."

The woman said, "I know the Messiah is coming—the one who is called Christ. When he comes, he will explain everything to us."

Then Jesus told her, "I Am the Messiah!"

Questions to think about

- Worship is so much more than singing! What are some other ways you can worship God this week?

- Are there areas in your life where you are more focused on yourself than on God? Why haven't you given those areas over to him?

- Jesus wants our worship to be authentic and real. List a few things you need to work on this week.

We think WE are the center of the universe. We think: Worship ME. But Jesus turns that all around and says that it isn't about us. He says: Worship ME.

Hanging out with God

It is SO much easier to live a life where the focus is on us! But Jesus flips so many things in our life around and challenges us to worship him. Find one of your favorite worship songs, and take a few moments to listen and worship God.

This space is here for you to jot down some thoughts, write out a prayer, draw a picture, or do whatever you want to help you remember your 10-minute moment:

DAY 8

READY TO PICK

I've never been a farmer, but I do have a certain understanding of how farming works. In school, for one of my classes we planted a little seed in a plastic foam cup and watched it grow. After carefully watering it and making sure it had enough sunlight, it wasn't long before a little green stem broke the surface. It was soon strong enough to take home. I proudly showed my mom, who tried to keep it alive as long as humanly possibly—while simultaneously hoping I would forget about it so that she could toss it out quietly when it inevitably died.

2 MINUTES

Scripture to read: John 4:34-38

Then Jesus explained: "My nourishment comes from doing the will of God, who sent me, and from finishing his work. You know the saying, 'Four months between planting and harvest.' But I say, wake up and look around. The fields are already ripe for harvest. The harvesters are paid good wages, and the fruit they harvest is people brought to eternal life. What joy awaits both the planter and the harvester alike! You know the saying, 'One plants and another harvests.' And it's true. I sent you to harvest where you didn't plant; others had already done the work, and now you will get to gather the harvest."

Questions to think about

- How have you been planting, watering, and shining light this week at your school?

- Have you ever seen someone's life change because you shared about Jesus Christ? How did that make you feel?

- The passage says that the harvest is ready—can you think of someone close to you, maybe in your own family, who is ready to trust in Jesus?

Sharing our faith is part of our mission. It would be a mistake to keep this to ourselves! When people see what Jesus has done in our lives, it should make others ask about that transformation. Your life is a constant testimony—be careful to live like a follower of Jesus today, because your actions are speaking loudly to those around you!

Hanging out with God

Think about three or four friends in your life who need to understand the forgiveness and love of Jesus Christ. Find some space on this page and write down their names; then pray for them this week. Ask God to have your lives cross and, if possible, to have a chance to share the good news of Jesus with them, too!

YOUR TURN

This space is here for you to jot down some thoughts, write out a prayer, draw a picture, or do whatever you want to help you remember your 10-minute moment:

DAY 9

SURRENDER!

When I was a kid, I loved LEGOS®. I'm glad I have kids now so I get to still play with them. Back in the day, I used to love building things and making something awesome out of a random pile of plastic bricks on the living room floor. Every month I would get a magazine that featured a Master Builder who could construct things with LEGOS I didn't think were possible. He built life-sized clones from Star Wars, giant skyscrapers, and starfighters that would give George Lucas a run for his money.

Building LEGOS in my own hands was fun and entertaining, but in the hands of a Master Builder the LEGO bricks turned into more than I could ever have imagined.

2 MINUTES

Scripture to read: John 6:8-14

Then Andrew, Simon Peter's brother, spoke up. "There's a young boy here with five barley loaves and two fish. But what good is that with this huge crowd?"

"Tell everyone to sit down," Jesus said. So they all sat down on the grassy slopes. (The men alone numbered about 5,000.) Then Jesus took the loaves, gave thanks to God, and distributed them to the people. Afterward he did the same with the fish. And they all ate as much as they wanted. After everyone was full, Jesus told his disciples, "Now gather the leftovers, so that nothing is wasted." So

they picked up the pieces and filled twelve baskets with scraps left by the people who had eaten from the five barley loaves.

When the people saw him do this miraculous sign, they exclaimed, "Surely, he is the Prophet we have been expecting!"

Questions to think about

- Jesus took care of these people, even with their most basic needs. What does that say about him caring and providing for you?

- Do you have worries in your life that you need to hand over to God?

- What do you need to surrender into the hands of Jesus today?

Hanging out with God

Jesus did something miraculous with two pieces of bread and some fish. What do you think he could do with your life if you fully surrendered yourself into his hands? Jesus is the master builder and can do so much more than we could ever imagine if we place our life into his hands. Take some time today to celebrate how Jesus is building and shaping your life for his work as you surrender to him.

YOUR TURN

This space is here for you to jot down some thoughts, write out a prayer, draw a picture, or do whatever you want to help you remember your 10-minute moment:

DAY 10

I AM HERE

I was on a cruise recently, and it was an incredible trip! There were all-you-can-eat buffets that were open all hours of the night, lots of fun and games, and great company. But life on the water isn't always fun and games. In today's passage the disciples are in a boat and freaking out because the water is rising and they are afraid for their lives.

2 MINUTES

Scripture to read: John 6:16-21

That evening Jesus' disciples went down to the shore to wait for him. But as darkness fell and Jesus still hadn't come back, they got into the boat and headed across the lake toward Capernaum. Soon a gale swept down upon them, and the sea grew very rough. They had rowed three or four miles when suddenly they saw Jesus walking on the water toward the boat. They were terrified, but he called out to them, "Don't be afraid. I am here!" Then they were eager to let him in the boat, and immediately they arrived at their destination!

Questions to think about

- Jesus' disciples were afraid and terrified even though he was with them physically. What freaks you out? Is there something in your life that makes it hard for you to trust in the Lord?

- Sometimes the waters in life can get pretty choppy. Is there a storm in your life that you need to confront or ask for Jesus' help to overcome?

- I like to panic. When things get tough, what is usually your first response?

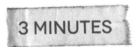

Hanging out with God

Storms in life are inevitable. Sometimes the only thing you can hold on to is the side of the boat—until God shows up. Ask God today to show up in your storms, call out to him, and be reassured of his calming voice saying, "Do not be afraid."

YOUR TURN

This space is here for you to jot down some thoughts, write out a prayer, draw a picture, or do whatever you want to help you remember your 10-minute moment:

DAY
11

NEVER LET YOU GO

Jesus compares himself to bread and water in today's passage. Both of these are essential to life! The best part of the life God intends us to live is that once we receive him he never lets us go.

We all fall short, we all fail and sin, but God's Spirit seals us until he returns to Earth.

2 MINUTES

Scripture to read: John 6:35-40

Jesus replied, "I am the bread of life. Whoever comes to me will never be hungry again. Whoever believes in me will never be thirsty. But you haven't believed in me even though you have seen me. However, those the Father has given me will come to me, and I will never reject them. For I have come down from heaven to do the will of God who sent me, not to do my own will. And this is the will of God, that I should not lose even one of all those he has given me, but that I should raise them up at the last day. For it is my Father's will that all who see his Son and believe in him should have eternal life. I will raise them up at the last day."

5 MINUTES

Questions to think about

- Bread and water are essential for life. How else does this metaphor hold up in comparison to Jesus? Do you live as if the Lord is essential in your life?

- Have you ever been rejected before? How did that make you feel?

- How exciting is it to think that someday followers of Jesus will get to spend eternity with him? When do you think that will happen?

3 MINUTES

Hanging out with God

As you eat bread today and drink water, thank God for the life he has given you, and commit to making it count. Make a commitment that until he returns you'll be faithful and devoted to the ways and teachings of his Son, Jesus.

This space is here for you to jot down some thoughts, write out a prayer, draw a picture, or do whatever you want to help you remember your 10-minute moment:

DAY
12

GO AND SIN NO MORE

Every time I hear a speaker talk about sin, I have something pretty specific that jumps right into my mind. I don't have to think very much about it—we all know the big places where we fall short.

Can you imagine your sins being on display in front of a large crowd? My sins up on the JumboTron®? Not my idea of a fun time at the baseball stadium. It would be the most humiliating event in the whole word! This is exactly what happens to a woman who was brought before Jesus.

2 MINUTES

Scripture to read: John 8:4-11

"Teacher," they said to Jesus, "this woman was caught in the act of adultery. The law of Moses says to stone her. What do you say?"

They were trying to trap him into saying something they could use against him, but Jesus stooped down and wrote in the dust with his finger. They kept demanding an answer, so he stood up again and said, "All right, but let the one who has never sinned throw the first stone!" Then he stooped down again and wrote in the dust.

When the accusers heard this, they slipped away one by one, beginning with the oldest, until only Jesus was left in the middle of the crowd with the woman. Then Jesus stood up again and said to the woman, "Where are your accusers? Didn't even one of them condemn you?"

"No, Lord," she said.

And Jesus said, "Neither do I. Go and sin no more."

Questions to think about

- This unnamed woman must have been humiliated. Has a sin of yours ever been exposed and embarrassed you?

- We don't know what Jesus wrote down in the dust. What do you think it might have said?

- The key here is to not continue in sin. Jesus says, "Go and sin no more." What sin are you most struggling with? Are you getting help to overcome it?

Hanging out with God

Jesus isn't encouraging anyone to sin or condoning this particular woman's actions at all. He is saying is that until we are in heaven, we won't be complete. We will always battle our fallen nature while we are in this world. The key is to keep fighting this battle and persevering against sin. When you stop fighting the battle against sin, the war is all but over. Make sure you seek good accountability with a friend, parent, or mentor to avoid unhealthy habits than can turn into a destructive lifestyle.

This space is here for you to jot down some thoughts, write out a prayer, draw a picture, or do whatever you want to help you remember your 10-minute moment:

DAY 13

I ONCE WAS BLIND

Jesus was a funny guy! In this passage he heals a man who was blind, by spitting into the ground and making mud pies for his eyes! Only Jesus would do something like that—using mud just to show he was the source of the healing and nothing else.

Today's passage takes place right after the blind man was healed, and he teaches us a valuable lesson…

2 MINUTES

Scripture to read: John 9:30-33

"Why, that's very strange!" the man replied. "He healed my eyes, and yet you don't know where he comes from? We know that God doesn't listen to sinners, but he is ready to hear those who worship him and do his will. Ever since the world began, no one has been able to open the eyes of someone born blind. If this man were not from God, he couldn't have done it."

Questions to think about

- Worship is more than a song—prayer is a vital part of worship as well. Do you pray regularly, or is it an afterthought?

- If Jesus had healed your eyes, what would have been your first reaction?

- How do you think you can improve your prayer life?

Hanging out with God

This man Jesus is from God! Not just that—he *is* God! Today spend extra time in prayer and talk to Jesus about what is on your heart. God is listening to your prayers and is ready to answer you according to his will. We don't understand everything in God's plan, but we can trust him. Today, know that God hears you, heals you, and wants what's best for your life.

YOUR TURN

This space is here for you to jot down some thoughts, write out a prayer, draw a picture, or do whatever you want to help you remember your 10-minute moment:

DAY 14

DUMB AS A TRUCK

I don't know much, but here's what I know about sheep:
- They are dumb as a truck
- I like clothes made from their wool
- They are dumb as a truck

When Jesus says that he protects his sheep from wolves and that he knows us and loves us, I'm so thankful for that! Even though I think I've figured out this life pretty well, I need to trust in him daily. I need to consciously remind myself that I need him and his ways to make sure that I safely navigate life. Listen to his voice, trust the shepherd, and don't be as dumb as a truck.

2 MINUTES

Scripture to read: John 10:11-18

"I am the good shepherd. The good shepherd sacrifices his life for the sheep. A hired hand will run when he sees a wolf coming. He will abandon the sheep because they don't belong to him and he isn't their shepherd. And so the wolf attacks them and scatters the flock. The hired hand runs away because he's working only for the money and doesn't really care about the sheep.

"I am the good shepherd; I know my own sheep, and they know me, just as my Father knows me and I know the Father. So I sacrifice my life for the sheep. I have other sheep, too, that are not in this sheepfold. I must bring them also. They will listen to my voice, and there will be one flock with one shepherd.

"The Father loves me because I sacrifice my life so I may take it back again. No one can take my life from me. I sacrifice it voluntarily. For I have the authority to lay it down when I want to and also to take it up again. For this is what my Father has commanded."

Questions to think about

- In what areas of your life are you resisting following Jesus' voice or plan for your life?

- What wolves (or temptations) are attacking you? Are these temptations drawing you away from God's protection?

- In being honest with yourself before God today, where are you being as dumb as a truck?

Too often we think we know what we're doing and have it all figured out. That is a dangerous place! If you start to rely on yourself, you will begin to wander and trust your path over God's path. Be careful!

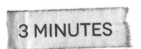

Hanging out with God

If you wander outside of the sheepfold and the sound of God's voice, you are in a dangerous place. Take some time today to talk with your parents or your youth leader about some of the struggles you are facing, and ask them for help to return to the safety of God's voice.

YOUR TURN

This space is here for you to jot down some thoughts, write out a prayer, draw a picture, or do whatever you want to help you remember your 10-minute moment:

DAY 15

FOREVER YOUNG

Imagine what it would be like to live forever. Even at just a few hundred years old, you would have seen the Civil War, the introduction of electricity into homes, the airplane, the Internet, and the iPhone®. As crazy as that would be, did you know that as a follower of Jesus you will live forever? Well, your body will die at some point—but Jesus promised an eternal life with him forever in heaven for those who accept his gift of salvation. How incredible is that?

2 MINUTES

Scripture to read: John 11:25-26

Jesus told her, "I am the resurrection and the life. Anyone who believes in me will live, even after dying. Everyone who lives in me and believes in me will never ever die. Do you believe this, Martha?"

5 MINUTES

Questions to think about

- If you could live at some point in the past, what century would you choose? Why?

- What is going to be your mark for Christ on the world in your limited time here on this earth?

- Do you truly believe that Jesus is the resurrection and the life?

Those who are followers of Jesus are going to live forever in God's presence. If you have lost a loved one in the past who was a Christ-follower, the Bible teaches that someday you will be reunited with that person in heaven. What an incredible comfort this is!

3 MINUTES

Hanging out with God

Take some time today to talk with someone older and wiser than you. Ask that person for some wisdom God has taught him or her over the years. Make sure that every day of your life counts. Since we don't know how long we have here on this earth, make sure you spend your time here wisely. Love God, love others, encourage people, build people up, and live without regrets. Live the way Jesus intended until someday we will be with him!

YOUR TURN

This space is here for you to jot down some thoughts, write out a prayer, draw a picture, or do whatever you want to help you remember your 10-minute moment:

DAY 16

GROW ON YOUR OWN

Today we are passing the halfway mark in this book—you're doing great! What makes me most excited is the Scripture that we're studying today! During Jesus' life he challenged his followers to be disciples—ardent, devoted followers of God. By getting this far in the devotion, you are learning and applying so much to your life and growing on your own, just like he taught. Keep going!

2 MINUTES

Scripture to read: John 12:23-26

Jesus replied, "Now the time has come for the Son of Man to enter into his glory. I tell you the truth, unless a kernel of wheat is planted in the soil and dies, it remains alone. But its death will produce many new kernels—a plentiful harvest of new lives. Those who love their life in this world will lose it. Those who care nothing for their life in this world will keep it for eternity. Anyone who wants to be my disciple must follow me, because my servants must be where I am. And the Father will honor anyone who serves me."

5 MINUTES

Questions to think about

- Jesus challenges us to lose our life to find it. What do you think that means?

- If you give it away, you will find it—huh? That isn't super clear, but it's absolutely profound—explain it in your own words.

- In what one specific area are you slacking as a disciple of Christ?

The life of a disciple isn't easy—being dedicated and being a servant isn't natural. We have a tendency to wander (remember, sheep are as dumb as a truck) and do our own thing. I'm so excited you have made it through this lesson as a reminder of your own faithfulness in discipleship.

3 MINUTES

Hanging out with God

There are many ways that you can grow spiritually. You can grow through discipleship or personal time with Jesus, but a big part of your spiritual growth comes from your local Christian community. The Christian community can be something like church, small groups, or your youth group. Take some time today to thank the people who are walking through life with you:
- Shoot out a few quick texts right now
- Write out a "thank you" card
- Tell your small group leader how important he or she is to you this week when you meet

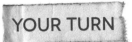

YOUR TURN

This space is here for you to jot down some thoughts, write out a prayer, draw a picture, or do whatever you want to help you remember your 10-minute moment:

DAY 17

DON'T THROW IN THE TOWEL

When I graduated from high school, my football coach gave me a really simple gift: a little hand towel. At first I thought he was just cheap, but then he explained his gift:

"Josh, don't ever be above serving. Don't ever get too self-important that you miss out on serving others. When you do that you become prideful and start to resist God using you for his work. Take up the towel and serve. Coach Price"

I've treasured that gift for many years now. While I've forgotten all of the other gifts given to me that week, I'll always keep that little towel and the lesson that it represents with me.

2 MINUTES

Scripture to read: John 13:12-17

After washing their feet, he put on his robe again and sat down and asked, "Do you understand what I was doing? You call me 'Teacher' and 'Lord,' and you are right, because that's what I am. And since I, your Lord and Teacher, have washed your feet, you ought to wash each other's feet. I have given you an example to follow. Do as I have done to you. I tell you the truth; slaves are not greater than their master. Nor is the messenger more important than the one who sends the message. Now that you know these things, God will bless you for doing them."

Questions to think about

- Where are you serving in your church or youth group?

- Servants are not greater than their master—if you are leading people you can only lead them where you have been. Are you consistently challenging yourself to grow on your own?

- Have you ever washed someone else's feet before? What would that experience be like for you?

Hanging out with God

We all like to BE served, but Jesus flips this on its head and challenges us to BE servants. Where can you find a place to serve? Where could you serve someone with kindness and a cheerful heart? God will bring many opportunities into your life to see if you are willing to serve others, so look for them today!

YOUR TURN

This space is here for you to jot down some thoughts, write out a prayer, draw a picture, or do whatever you want to help you remember your 10-minute moment:

DAY 18

LOVE WINS

Certain people are really tough to love. They are so stubborn and challenging that it almost seems that they do not deserve our love. In fact, in writing that last sentence, the name of that person in my life came right to mind. Did that happen to you, too, as you read what I wrote?

Jesus challenges us to love everyone completely, even the person or people that you are thinking about right now—even when it seems impossible. You see, when you love people—even the tough ones—you are showing that you are a follower of Jesus.

Scripture to read: John 13:34-35

"So now I am giving you a new commandment: Love each other. Just as I have loved you, you should love each other. Your love for one another will prove to the world that you are my disciples."

5 MINUTES

Questions to think about

- Who are your favorite people in your Christian community? Why are they so important to you?

- Who is that person who grates you the wrong way? What would it take for you to love him or her?

- How does it feel when someone doesn't love you?

3 MINUTES

Hanging out with God

Your love for one another will prove that you are Jesus' disciples— and the opposite is true as well. When we hold grudges, bully, hate, or discriminate, we turn people off to our faith. Think through your circles of friends, and discover where you need to make some changes.

- Is there someone I intentionally leave out of things?
- Where am I a bully to someone?
- Who have I still not forgiven for something they did that hurt me?

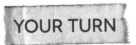

YOUR TURN

This space is here for you to jot down some thoughts, write out
a prayer, draw a picture, or do whatever you want to help you
remember your 10-minute moment:

DAY 19

DENIED ACCESS

Living for Jesus isn't an easy journey—there are successes and failures, wins and losses. Maybe recently you have fallen away from God or have struggled with an addiction or sin. This is normal! Don't freak out—just fight through it, find forgiveness, and walk back into the Lord's forgiving and accepting embrace. God wants the absolute best for your life. Don't let your struggles conquer you, and don't let being trapped in sin continue another day.

2 MINUTES

Scripture to read: John 13:36-38

Simon Peter asked, "Lord, where are you going?"

And Jesus replied, "You can't go with me now, but you will follow me later."

"But why can't I come now, Lord?" he asked. "I'm ready to die for you."

Jesus answered, "Die for me? I tell you the truth, Peter—before the rooster crows tomorrow morning, you will deny three times that you even know me."

Questions to think about

- Where have you fallen short in your walk with the Lord this week?

- Do you have an accountability partner? If so, why did you pick that person? If not, have you thought about getting one?

- Have you confessed your sins to both God and someone else who can help you? Invite that person to walk with you when you go through hard times!

Hanging out with God

Peter thought he was ready for the trials, but there was a big test that he clearly failed by denying Jesus not once, but three times! He would go on to do incredible things for Jesus and became one of the founders of the early church. However, he went through times of failure and denial and walked far from Christ. If you are struggling today, don't give up hope—walk back to Jesus and into the great things he has planned for your life.

YOUR TURN

This space is here for you to jot down some thoughts, write out a prayer, draw a picture, or do whatever you want to help you remember your 10-minute moment:

DAY 20

ONE-WAY STREET

I remember one time driving down the highway and seeing headlights coming the wrong way down the road—right toward us! We slowed down, pulled off to the side of the road, and waited for this sweet old lady to pass. She had driven up a "do not enter" off-ramp and freaked everyone out by coming at them head-on. She had taken a wrong turn and was definitely headed in the wrong direction.

According to the Bible, all roads don't lead to heaven—there are roads that are heading the wrong direction, too!

2 MINUTES

Scripture to read: John 14:1-6

"Don't let your hearts be troubled. Trust in God, and trust also in me. There is more than enough room in my Father's home. If this were not so, would I have told you that I am going to prepare a place for you? When everything is ready, I will come and get you, so that you will always be with me where I am. And you know the way to where I am going."

"No, we don't know, Lord," Thomas said. "We have no idea where you are going, so how can we know the way?"

Jesus told him, "I am the way, the truth, and the life. No one can come to the Father except through me."

5 MINUTES

Questions to think about

- Is the Bible clear there is only one way to heaven? Why or why not?

- Why is this teaching so unpopular? Do you feel that we are encouraged to be tolerant? Have you ever been told that all roads lead to heaven? After reading this Scripture, do you think this idea is true?

- What is most exciting to you about heaven?

You can't earn your way there.
You can't be good enough.
You can't be smart enough.
Fast-talkers can't talk their way in.
Everyone just doesn't go there automatically.
There is only one way to heaven. Through Jesus Christ.

3 MINUTES

Hanging out with God

This isn't exactly a popular thing to say today, but if you believe in Jesus then you have to trust his words. There is ONE WAY to heaven, and the way there is through the Son of God. We should be good, we should be kind, and we should help others—good works should mark our lives as a result of a life sold out to him. But we can't earn our way to heaven because of those good works.

Take a few moments before you start your day today and thank God for his salvation. Share the "one way" message with someone else, too!

YOUR TURN

This space is here for you to jot down some thoughts, write out a prayer, draw a picture, or do whatever you want to help you remember your 10-minute moment:

DAY 21

CONNECTION LOST

I am always connected. I never leave home without my iPhone, making me instantly connected to everything. If someone posts a picture or needs to get ahold of me, I'm right there. My phone is constantly vibrating in my pocket, alerting me to what is going on. Almost not a moment goes by where I'm not online, and when I get disconnected, I don't like it for one second!

There's something unhealthy about that when it comes to technology, but something awesome happens when we live like that with Christ.

2 MINUTES

Scripture to read: John 15:1-8

"I am the true grapevine, and my Father is the gardener. He cuts off every branch of mine that doesn't produce fruit, and he prunes the branches that do bear fruit so they will produce even more. You have already been pruned and purified by the message I have given you. Remain in me, and I will remain in you. For a branch cannot produce fruit if it is severed from the vine, and you cannot be fruitful unless you remain in me.

"Yes, I am the vine; you are the branches. Those who remain in me, and I in them, will produce much fruit. For apart from me you can do nothing. Anyone who does not remain in me is thrown away like a useless branch and withers. Such branches are gathered into a pile to be burned. But if you remain in me and my words remain in you,

you may ask for anything you want, and it will be granted! When you produce much fruit, you are my true disciples. This brings great glory to my Father."

Questions to think about

- How would you feel if you were disconnected from your phone or the Internet for a full day?

- How easy is it to fake that we are connected to Jesus? In what areas do you do that?

- What steps can you take this week to make sure you stay connected to Jesus? Who can help you live this way?

If the Bible were written today, it would talk about us being online and connected to each other and the Internet. But instead of apps and laptops, it uses a vine and branches to illustrate our need for a connection to God at all times.

Hanging out with God

Commit in your heart today to be as connected to the Lord as you are to technology. I couldn't go a day without looking at my gadgets—make sure you don't go too long without being connected to him, either.

YOUR TURN

This space is here for you to jot down some thoughts, write out a prayer, draw a picture, or do whatever you want to help you remember your 10-minute moment:

DAY
22

JUDGMENT DAY

I've never had the distinction of having to stand before a judge before. I've come close: I've witnessed a car accident before and thought they would call me but ended up settling out of court. I've been picked for jury duty but haven't ever actually made it into the courtroom.

But someday I will stand before a judge, and he will judge me for what I've done. But instead of seeing my sins, failures, and faults, God will see the forgiveness of Jesus Christ.

2 MINUTES

Scripture to read: John 16:5-11

"But now I am going away to the one who sent me, and not one of you is asking where I am going. Instead, you grieve because of what I've told you. But in fact, it is best for you that I go away, because if I don't, the Advocate won't come. If I do go away, then I will send him to you. And when he comes, he will convict the world of its sin, and of God's righteousness, and of the coming judgment. The world's sin is that it refuses to believe in me. Righteousness is available because I go to the Father, and you will see me no more. Judgment will come because the ruler of this world has already been judged."

5 MINUTES

Questions to think about

- Have you thanked God for the Advocate (the Holy Spirit), who lives inside of you and guides you each day?

- With what urgency are you sharing the message of Jesus with this sinful world?

- What can you do to improve God's name in your school, community, or youth group?

3 MINUTES

Hanging out with God

Being judged isn't fun for anyone—and we get to escape the eternal penalty of our sin because of God's forgiveness through Jesus Christ. Don't let that be a license to sin—that isn't what he intends at all. Live your life for Christ, and realize that what you do has a great effect on others who are already feeling judged and desperately seeking him.

YOUR TURN

This space is here for you to jot down some thoughts, write out a prayer, draw a picture, or do whatever you want to help you remember your 10-minute moment:

DAY 23

TRIALS HD

The Christian life isn't easy! Many people who trust Jesus as their Savior incorrectly believe that life is going to be easy street from here on out. But it simply isn't true—and Jesus warns us about this false thinking. This life will be challenging, but don't worry: He is totally in control.

2 MINUTES

Scripture to read: John 16:31-33

Jesus asked, "Do you finally believe? But the time is coming—indeed it's here now—when you will be scattered, each one going his own way, leaving me alone. Yet I am not alone because the Father is with me. I have told you all this so that you may have peace in me. Here on earth you will have many trials and sorrows. But take heart, because I have overcome the world."

5 MINUTES

Questions to think about

- What are some of the trials and struggles you have faced this past year?

- Where do you go or to whom do you turn when things turn ugly in your life?

- Have you ever faced persecution for what you believe?

3 MINUTES

Hanging out with God

Trials and sorrows usually turn into a test of our faith. They are often very challenging and leave us unsettled because we were expecting something easier. If things are good—trust God and build up a strong faith now before it turns the other direction. And if things are really tough right now—hang in there and remember that God knows where you are and has everything under control.

This space is here for you to jot down some thoughts, write out a prayer, draw a picture, or do whatever you want to help you remember your 10-minute moment:

DAY 24

ALL FOR ONE

There is nothing more destructive to a church, youth group, or friendship than gossip. When we undermine each other, we hurt the foundation of our cause and negate the mission we are called to accomplish. What would it look like if we were all united as one? One faith, one love, one mission?

That's the type of faith and community Jesus intended us to have. Today we look at his words as a vision for what the church can be.

2 MINUTES

Scripture to read: John 17:20-21

"I am praying not only for these disciples but also for all who will ever believe in me through their message. I pray that they will all be one, just as you and I are one—as you are in me, Father, and I am in you. And may they be in us so that the world will believe you sent me."

5 MINUTES

Questions to think about

- Have you ever hurt a friend or damaged a relationship?

- What can you do to repair any damage you may have caused?

- What would it look like if we were all for one and one for all?

The Three Musketeers made the statement "All for one, one for all" famous, but there is a ton of truth to having each other's backs! Who can you help defend this week? What can you do to maintain the integrity of Christ's church?

3 MINUTES

Hanging out with God

Commit today to only be a part of the solution, not the problem, and to be unified with the vision and mission of your church. Stop gossip in its tracks. The more you are involved and engaged, the more you will help in defending your church, relationship, or youth group. It is usually people on the fringes of the faith that undermine the church the most. Make a commitment: Go all in. Go all for one and one for all.

YOUR TURN

This space is here for you to jot down some thoughts, write out a prayer, draw a picture, or do whatever you want to help you remember your 10-minute moment:

DAY 25

THE SECRET DISCIPLE

Have you ever been ashamed or embarrassed of your faith? It happens to all of us from time to time—either someone who claims to be a Christ-follower does something that wasn't great, or maybe you're with a group or people and Jesus is being ridiculed. Either way, it isn't easy to stand for your faith and stand up at a critical time.

2 MINUTES

Scripture to read: John 19:38-42

Afterward Joseph of Arimathea, who had been a secret disciple of Jesus (because he feared the Jewish leaders), asked Pilate for permission to take down Jesus' body. When Pilate gave permission, Joseph came and took the body away. With him came Nicodemus, the man who had come to Jesus at night. He brought about seventy-five pounds of perfumed ointment made from myrrh and aloes. Following Jewish burial custom, they wrapped Jesus' body with the spices in long sheets of linen cloth. The place of crucifixion was near a garden, where there was a new tomb, never used before. And so, because it was the day of preparation for the Jewish Passover and since the tomb was close at hand, they laid Jesus there.

5 MINUTES

Questions to think about

- Joseph of Arimathea had been fearful of what others would think. When are you most ashamed of being a Christian?

- Nicodemus (the same guy from Day 6) had come to Jesus by night but now came into the open. Why do you think that changed?

- What would it take for you to openly and honestly stand for Jesus Christ every day?

3 MINUTES

Hanging out with God

Jesus did so much for us on the cross. The cross is one of the most significant icons of Christianity, but it is more than just a symbol to wear around your neck or an image to decorate a sanctuary. The cross is where our sins were laid on Christ and where he substituted himself for our sins. Joseph and Nicodemus finally realized what happened when Jesus died and came alive. In your prayer time today, pray to live up to their standard and to lift high the cross of Jesus.

YOUR TURN

This space is here for you to jot down some thoughts, write out a prayer, draw a picture, or do whatever you want to help you remember your 10-minute moment:

DAY 26

BACK TO LIFE

Every Easter, churches are packed and sometimes overflowing with people. This is partly because going to church on Easter is a cultural tradition (just like the huge influx of people that attend Christmas services), but part of it is also a respect for what is one of the most important tenets of the Christian faith.

You see, if Jesus stayed dead, then it would prove he wasn't really God's Son. The resurrection of Jesus is one of the most critical aspects of Christianity. Let's read about it today:

2 MINUTES

Scripture to read: John 20:1-9

Early on Sunday morning, while it was still dark, Mary Magdalene came to the tomb and found that the stone had been rolled away from the entrance. She ran and found Simon Peter and the other disciple, the one whom Jesus loved. She said, "They have taken the Lord's body out of the tomb, and we don't know where they have put him!"

Peter and the other disciple started out for the tomb. They were both running, but the other disciple outran Peter and reached the tomb first. He stooped and looked in and saw the linen wrappings lying there, but he didn't go in. Then Simon Peter arrived and went inside. He also noticed the linen wrappings lying there, while the cloth that had covered Jesus' head was folded up and lying apart from the other wrappings. Then the disciple who had reached the tomb first also went in, and he saw and believed—for until then they still hadn't understood the Scriptures that said Jesus must rise from the dead.

Questions to think about

- If Jesus is more powerful than even death, what does it say about him understanding your problems and pain?

- What would your reaction have been to the empty tomb if you were the first person there?

- What is the significance in the resurrection of Jesus to you?

Hanging out with God

Don't let Christmas and Easter become the only times you go to church! Gathering as a church is vitally important to the life of a Christ-follower and critical to make sure you are growing in your faith and being held accountable as a follower of Jesus. Churches all around the world every year celebrate the resurrection of Jesus every weekend! Commit to being a faithful member of a local church body from now on (if you aren't already).

YOUR TURN

This space is here for you to jot down some thoughts, write out a prayer, draw a picture, or do whatever you want to help you remember your 10-minute moment:

DAY 27

I DOUBT IT

When I was a teenager, I had doubts about the whole Jesus thing.

But I had said I was a follower of Jesus, so I was too embarrassed to say anything about it. But it didn't go away—in fact, some things piled up, and pretty soon I found myself in a crisis of faith that took a few years to work through.

What I love about the passage you're about to read is that Thomas didn't hesitate to share his doubts. He just spilled them out there, and in the process, his searching led him to some life-changing answers. Be honest about your doubts, and look for some substantial answers to ground your faith solidly.

2 MINUTES

Scripture to read: John 20:24-29

One of the twelve disciples, Thomas (nicknamed the Twin), was not with the others when Jesus came. They told him, "We have seen the Lord!"

But he replied, "I won't believe it unless I see the nail wounds in his hands, put my fingers into them, and place my hand into the wound in his side."

Eight days later the disciples were together again, and this time Thomas was with them. The doors were locked; but suddenly, as before, Jesus was standing among them. "Peace be with you," he said. Then he said to Thomas, "Put your finger here, and look at my hands. Put your hand into the wound in my side. Don't be faithless any longer. Believe!"

"My Lord and my God!" Thomas exclaimed.

Then Jesus told him, "You believe because you have seen me. Blessed are those who believe without seeing me."

Questions to think about

- What passages in the Bible are hard for you to believe? Why?

- Are you struggling to reconcile what you know about God with something that is happening in your life? If so, what is it?

- Oftentimes walking through doubt with someone else will help you find the other side of it. Who is there for you when you need them in times like that?

Thomas got a tough nickname: Doubting Thomas. But his doubt and eventual belief led him to an incredible depth of his faith in Jesus Christ. He believed so fervently that he took the good news of Jesus to the ends of the earth before being martyred for his faith. We should start a campaign to get his nickname changed to Devoted Thomas—because that's exactly what he became.

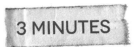

3 MINUTES

Hanging out with God

Doubt is a normal and acceptable part of our lives. Anyone who says they don't ever doubt is lying. We all wonder from time to time if something in the Bible is true or makes sense—if you don't admit to this insecurity and seek to find answers to your questions, the doubts and uncertainties will begin to nag at you and will eventually undermine your faith. The answers are out there, so don't wait—and find someone you can talk to today so that you can walk through your doubts together!

YOUR TURN

This space is here for you to jot down some thoughts, write out a prayer, draw a picture, or do whatever you want to help you remember your 10-minute moment:

DAY 28

I'VE GOT THE POWER

I'm constantly monitoring the remaining battery percentage on my phone. There's nothing more frustrating than running out of battery at the wrong time—right when you're expecting an important message, or when you need to call your mom and let her know you're running late for curfew.

What about God's power? It doesn't run out, but we must be constantly plugged in to stay fully charged.

2 MINUTES

Scripture to read: John 20:30-31

The disciples saw Jesus do many other miraculous signs in addition to the ones recorded in this book. But these are written so that you may continue to believe that Jesus is the Messiah, the Son of God, and that by believing in him you will have life by the power of his name.

5 MINUTES

Questions to think about

- When do you feel the most spiritually drained?

- What do you do to stay recharged with God?

- If you could serve in some way in your church or community and knew you wouldn't fail, what would you do?

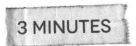

3 MINUTES

Hanging out with God

God wants to use you in the same way that the disciples were used to spread the good news of Jesus all over the world. God is going to do great things through you—but you have to be connected to God in order for him to work through you. God's power is limitless, but too often we limit it by thinking we've got it under control. Learn this now and it'll pay off with a lifetime of God's incredible power inside you!

YOUR TURN

This space is here for you to jot down some thoughts, write out a prayer, draw a picture, or do whatever you want to help you remember your 10-minute moment:

DAY 29

LOVE PEOPLE

A typical day in my world is as follows: My butler makes me a gourmet breakfast, and I have my driver take me to the movie theater. My chef prepares gourmet meals for me throughout the day, and my personal trainer guides me through my daily workout. I probably had you right up until the exercise part, right?

Yeah…then I wake up from my dream world! Here's reality: Although most of us don't have butlers, personal chefs, and drivers, we do live in an incredibly self-centered world. Jesus challenged that mindset and called us to live another way.

2 MINUTES

Scripture to read: John 21:15-17

After breakfast Jesus asked Simon Peter, "Simon son of John, do you love me more than these?"

"Yes, Lord," Peter replied, "you know I love you."

"Then feed my lambs," Jesus told him.

Jesus repeated the question: "Simon son of John, do you love me?"

"Yes, Lord," Peter said, "you know I love you."

"Then take care of my sheep," Jesus said.

A third time he asked him, "Simon son of John, do you love me?"

Questions to think about

- Once again we've got a sheep theme going! Why do you think this type of imagery comes up again?

- Why do you think Jesus questions Peter's love for him? What is Jesus asking Peter to do in this passage?

- Peter eventually became very passionate about the church. What can you do with your talents, gifts, and abilities for God's kingdom?

Hanging out with God

In the self-centered world we live in, it should be no surprise that most people live a life focused solely on themselves. People rarely look up from their busy lives to care for other people. It is even less common for people to give up their time or their money to help others. Let it be different among us! Let us be people who care for others, love each other, and give selflessly.

YOUR TURN

This space is here for you to jot down some thoughts, write out a prayer, draw a picture, or do whatever you want to help you remember your 10-minute moment:

THE REST OF THE STORY

You made it! Today is the last 10-minute moment in this volume. I'm proud of you for your faithfulness in spending time with God every day. The last Scripture today is the very last verse from the very last chapter of the book of John. Here it is—and congratulations!

Scripture to read: John 21:25

Jesus also did many other things. If they were all written down, I suppose the whole world could not contain the books that would be written.

5 MINUTES

Questions to think about

- How awesome is that verse! What else would you imagine Jesus doing while he walked on this earth?

- God's story is still continuing through you and your faithfulness. What will you commit to do for him from here?

- How can you share your commitment to the Lord with others?

3 MINUTES

Hanging out with God

Thank God for sending his Son, Jesus, to teach us so much but also to save us from our sins. Thank God for giving us his Spirit to guide us until someday we're with him in heaven. Thank God for the gift of his church, communion, and baptism. Ask God for strength and wisdom as you live your life to please him.

YOUR TURN

This space is here for you to jot down some thoughts, write out a prayer, draw a picture, or do whatever you want to help you remember your 10-minute moment: